CW01262312

TRACING THE RAINBOW

TRACING THE RAINBOW

Words from the heart to lift the soul and calm the mind

ANNE ADAMS

Published by Lindow Publishing

© Copyright 2005 by Anne Adams

All rights reserved.
No part of this publication may be reproduced, stored in a retrieval system, or transmitted, in any form or by any means, electronic, mechanical, photocopying, recording or otherwise,
without the prior permission of the Copyright Owner

ISBN: 0-95515 36-0-3

Printed and bound in Great Britain by Alpine Press Ltd
Kings Langley, Hertfordshire

In memory of my friend

Florence Healey

who gave me so much love and encouragement

O Joy that seekest me through pain,
I cannot close my heart to Thee:
I trace the rainbow through the rain,
And feel the promise is not vain
That morn shall tearless be.

G MATHESON

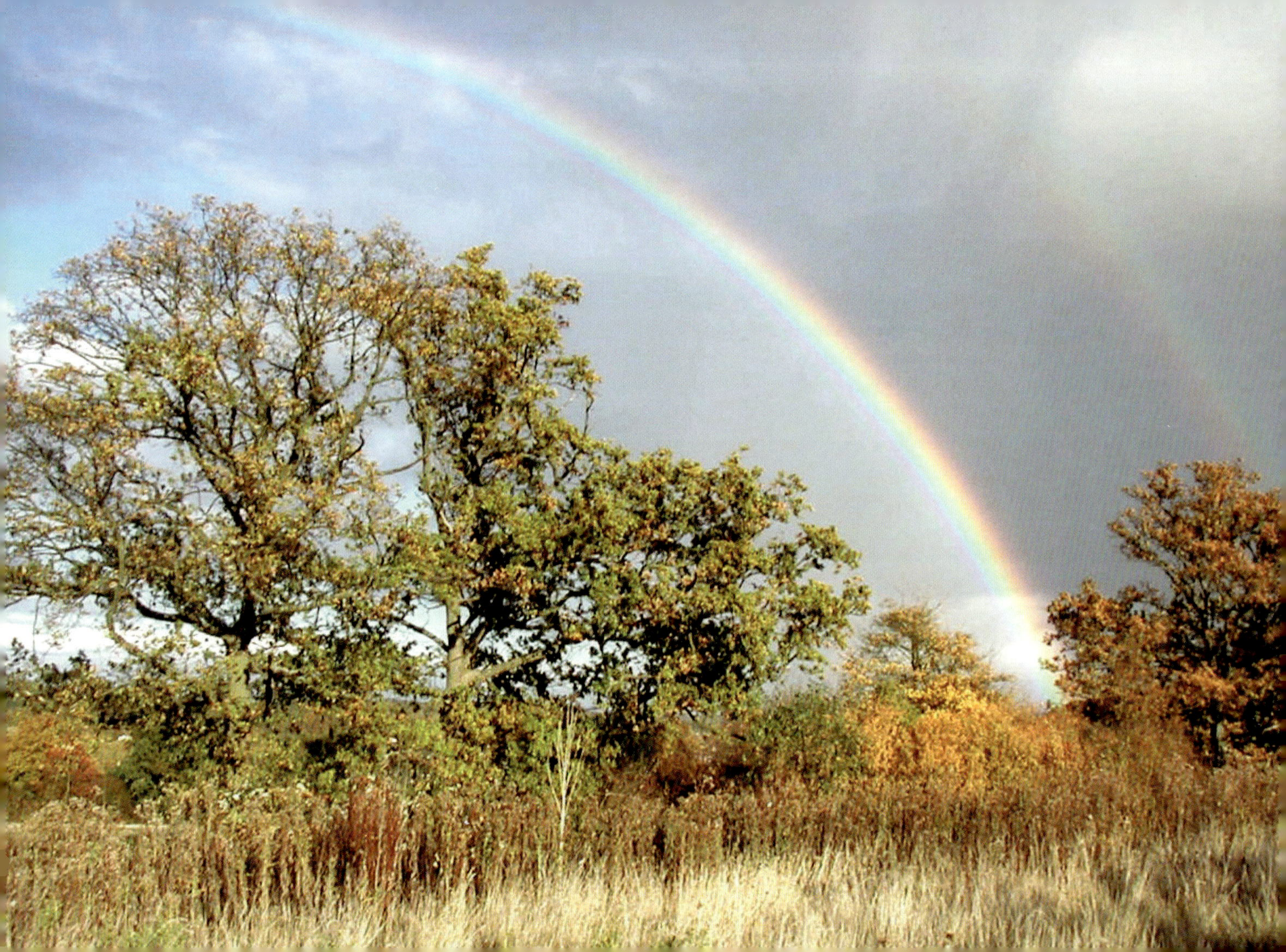

Foreword

*"The frisson you get from a fine line of poetry comes chiefly I think from the sheer pleasure that someone has recorded something that only **you** thought you had felt before." - Martyn Harris "Odd Man Out" (1996)*

Many words, stories and legends are told during the course of serious illness, but only this year I have discovered that poetry can often say so much more in far fewer words. "A short cut to the essential" . . . Poetry can capture complex emotions, human drama and natural wonders in a way that a paragraph never could. It is no coincidence that Apollo is both the God of Healing and the God of Poetry!

I have seen poetry be a comfort for the dying, enlightening for the living and illuminating for those of us learning - enjoy Anne's poems wherever they take you.

Dr Ros Taylor
Medical Director, Hospice of St Francis   September 2005

(Opposite is the double rainbow as it appeared over the site of the new Hospice in October 2004)

I record my grateful thanks for the generosity of:

> Alpine Press Limited
> Station Road
> Kings Langley
> Hertfordshire
> WD4 8LF

CONTENTS

Sensory Perception	13
A Celebration of the Seasons	15
Austrian Summer	37
Memories of Times Past	43
Light and joy	53

Sensory Perception

What is this light that flows in radiant streams
From azure seas by Heaven's cloudy shore?
Across the Earth its rays of glory pour
To lift the soul and fill our waking dreams.
One taste, one scent, can serve to stir the mind
And take us back in time to youthful days;
One touch, one look of love, can light a blaze,
And words can sway, be spiteful or be kind.
And cannot Music lift us on its wings
And carry us through lands of sounds divine,
Where trembling chords and soaring voice and line
Can hurt as much as when a skylark sings?
For joy and pain in Sense are intertwined
And tears released are calming to the mind.

A CELEBRATION OF THE SEASONS

A RING CYCLE OF SONNETS

January

As John the Baptist heralded the Son,
So fiery skies, the coming of our light.
Rose-garlanded, the azure sky looks on,
While climbs the gilded orb to end the night.
From northern wastes, a rushing, mighty blast
Sends scudding clouds across the frozen earth,
Where groaning trees their agued shadows cast
And whirling birds announce the sun's rebirth.
The huddled sheep await the tractor's drone,
Their fleeces burnished golden in the light,
And, where the autumn seeds were lately sown,
The gulls besport themselves in grey and white.
Thus, from this virgin January morn
Comes forth a child, a year just newly born.

And now the clouds pile purple in the west,
Advancing, like an army t'ward the sun:
Cold arrows pierce the country's airy breast,
'Til rivers burst and raging battle's done.
In new-found calm, the leaden skies retreat
And weakened rays shine on the distant peaks,
Which, white with snow, the Lakeland at their feet,
Rise up, serene, above the silent creeks.
Men come outdoors and greet the lightened skies,
And birds once more unfurl their folded wings:
Above the hedges and the roofs they rise
To celebrate the freshness of all things.
At length, the fiery, blood-red disc descends,
And, with its going, one day's glory ends.

February

How is it that the birds know when 'tis time
To pierce the darkness with their joyous song,
To waken men from dreams to sounds divine,
And fill the air with piping clear and strong?
Now yellow jasmine flowers for our delight
And snowdrops quiver by the garden wall;
New spears of green push upward to the light
And velvet pansies lift their faces small.
The golden willow stems are catkin-dressed
And green-barked trees are glowing in the lane.
For hopes of spring are burgeoning in the breast
And lovers know it's February again.
Let every youth for every maiden pine:
There is just one to be your Valentine.

March

As lions fight to keep their captured prey,
So March comes in and shakes his wintry mane.
New nests, high in the branches, lurch and sway,
And old leaves spin before the driving rain.
Just now and then the gentle lamb appears,
Elusive as the fleeting pastel sky,
And warms the cold-stoned graveyards, drenched with tears,
Where primroses in lemon clusters lie.
Sweet violets – white and purple – lie between,
And daffodils their silent trumpets blow;
The crocus spreads a carpet on the green
And blackthorn blossoms fill the air with snow.
The busy blue-tits hunt on tireless wing:
And thus does Nature welcome in the spring.

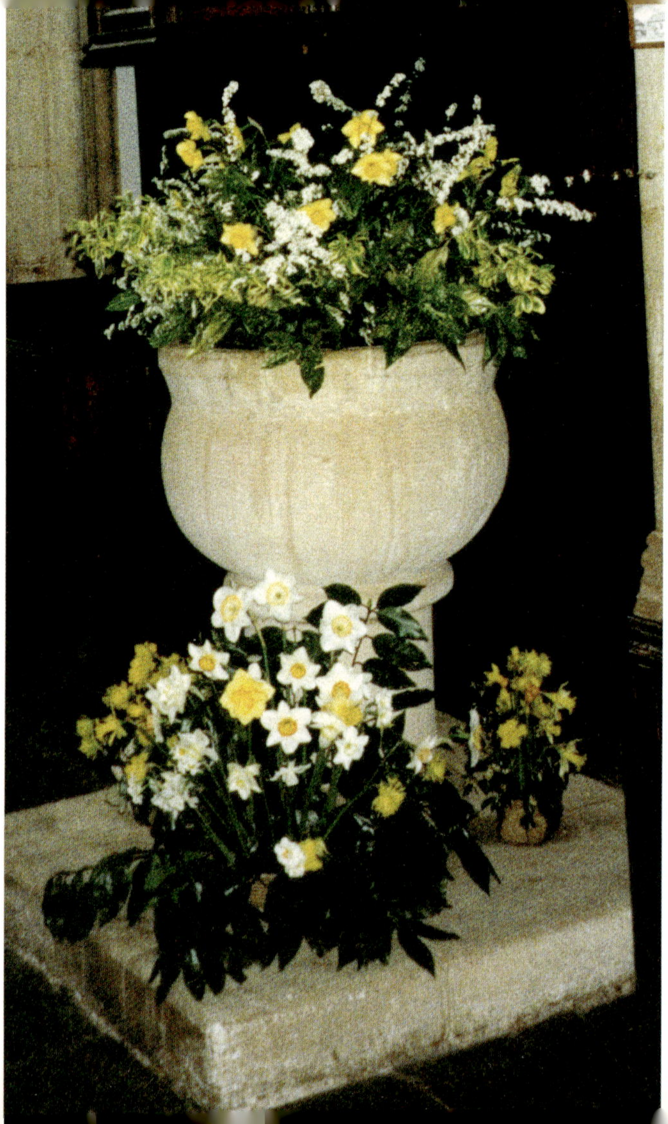

April

How welcome is the warmth, however brief,
That heats the clammy stones and dries the clay:
It breathes new life into each tender leaf
'Til shades of green have banished brown and grey.
The Easter lambs are gambolling on the hill
And ancient naves are bright with Easter flowers:
The fresh perfume pervades where all is still
And nothing heeds the passing of the hours.
Out in the open sky, the hazed clouds race
To cover up the sun with sudden rain,
And sunlit droplets fall like silver lace
Or slide like diamonds down the window pane.
And as each April miracle unfolds
The gardens fill with purples, reds and golds.

May

Now is the zenith of the Creator's power:
The palette tilts, the colours overflow.
Azaleas blaze and flaunt each pungent flower
While bluebells mist the shady earth below.
Wisteria flowers, in palest mauve, cascade
From ancient eaves down mellowed sandstone walls,
And rhododendrons 'jewel the dappled shade
And swathe the grassy walks of stately halls.
From out each blackbird's throat rich piping springs
To echo through the leafy canopies:
The thrush, amid the hawthorn blossom, sings,
And breezes stir the flowering chestnut trees.
For Spring's fair queen, the month of May, is here:
The most enchanting time in all our glorious year.

Tall trees with splendour now are dressed
In myriad greens, wine-red, and copper hues,
Their new-born leaves by gentle winds caressed
And daily drenched with chilly morning dews.
As brides prepared for church, the hedges stand,
Adorned with flowing trains of creamy lace;
They look upon the undulating land,
The stream within the wooded hills' embrace.
Knee-deep in buttercups, cows take their fill
And gather one by one beside the gate.
Then through and out across the road they spill
Where passers-by must pause awhile and wait.
High overhead, with twilight comes the moon
As, silently, sweet May slips into June.

June

The early mist gives way to cloudless skies
And sunshine glints from polished blades of grass,
And laurel leaves, and wings of butterflies,
That flit, and twist, and pause, then gently pass.
In city parks and gardens large and small,
On walls and trellises, in country lanes,
There stirs a flower, belovèd of us all,
An emblem of great battles and campaigns.
Above the smooth, barbed stem the green bud waits
'Til, warmed and ready, it begins to swell:
A conch of velvet silently rotates
Revealing richest colours; wondrous smell
And heady heat hangs heavy in the rooms
Where vases overflow with Summer blooms.

Now beauty fades from ev'ry hanging leaf
As each one dulls and darkens on its stem:
The drying heat has crept up like a thief
To steal the freshness out of each of them.
And yet the wheat is ranked in muted green
And stands with every spear-point raised on high;
And silken scarlet poppies can be seen,
Like banners trembling 'neath the denim sky.
The ox-eye daisy, in its millions, grows
By motorways and tangled hedges fair;
The honeysuckle mingles with the rose:
Mock orange blossom fills the sultry air.
Come, look and see! As lingering daylight dies,
The bats fly through the opalescent skies.

July

The hay is cut and grass-scent fills the air,
While naked sheep proclaim their loss aloud.
Convolvulus sends out its trumpets fair;
The rose bay willow herb stands tall and proud.
An anvil towers above the humid earth
And hazy clouds blot out the blazing light;
The rumbling giant, Thor, gives way to mirth
As Zeus strikes lightning bolts for his delight.
Hailstones, like pearls unstrung, transform the scene
To winter white: until the flooding rain
Makes rivers flow where once the roads have been
And, sun restored, the storm begins to wane.
The vapours then rise up on unseen wings
As Earth, refreshed, gives back what Nature brings.

Dune grasses rustle in the morning breeze
And sunlight sparkles on a cobalt sea.
White campion lies in waiting for the bees
And white-flowered brambles lengthen silently.
From out the corn the skylarks rise and sing
Such songs of heavenly music to our ears,
We stand entranced, as each small feathered thing
Soars up into the blue and disappears.
Only the songs remain upon the air,
To draw away our ears from mortal noise,
As if those songs had turned into a prayer
And we had caught a glimpse of Heaven's joys.
And so July, in heat and beauty, dies,
And August rules the realm of Summer skies.

August

Sun-baked, the cornfields lie like golden sand
Amid the patchwork vales and woodlands fair.
Wild flowers bloom in heath and meadowland
And insects drone and drift through drowsy air.
The buddleia is crowned with butterflies,
The mountain ash with fruit is all ablaze,
The fell, no longer dark and brooding lies,
But, purple-dressed, its beauty now displays.
The gentle breeze sends silken seeds aloft
To spin and shine like finest silver stars
Above a crowded street or lonely croft,
By sparkling streams and rippling reservoirs.
In leafy lanes the harvesters go by
And plundered fields are open to the sky.

September

September brings a magic of its own:
A whitened sun, that feigns its summer heat,
A dampness seeping into soil and stone,
And tousled ferns and nettles at our feet.
In early morn the mist begins to rise
Like wreaths of smoke, but caught, and stilled, and held,
Completely white, mysterious, opaque,
Until, by warming beams, it is dispelled.
Trimmed hedges snake their way through green and brown
With twisted limbs stripped naked to the bone,
And elders hang their jet-black berries down
Where once their virgin creamy flowers have grown.
And hips and haws, in red and orange gleam,
And trembling leaves are changed, as in a dream.

October

See how the sun and rain and frost conspire
To weave a magic spell for our delight:
For when the damp and cold are mixed with fire
Then leaves and ferns and creepers all ignite.
When scarlet rags of cloud burn in the west
And stars peep out from dusky turquoise light,
The frost descends and, like a thing possessed,
Bedecks the world below in frosty white.
But, when the morning sun in strength returns,
It sets that stiff and frozen world ablaze:
Against the blue each leafy tree-top burns,
Reflecting glory from the warming rays.
And amber, gold, deep pink and red and wine
By placid pools in double beauty shine.

The new-ploughed fields glow in the early light
Like pink-brown flesh beneath a salmon's skin;
Tree shadows, stark and doubling their height,
Across the green stretch black and paper-thin.
Great arrowheads of geese pierce grey-washed skies
And flocks of birds are moving now as one:
Like shoals of fish in corralled paradise,
They swoop and twist and turn and then are gone.
The summer blooms have lost their vibrancy,
Now purple daisies glisten in the rain,
And autumn pansies, in their infancy,
Spread out their roots where other roots have lain.
On stealthy feet, October makes his way:
A month of change, of glory and decay.

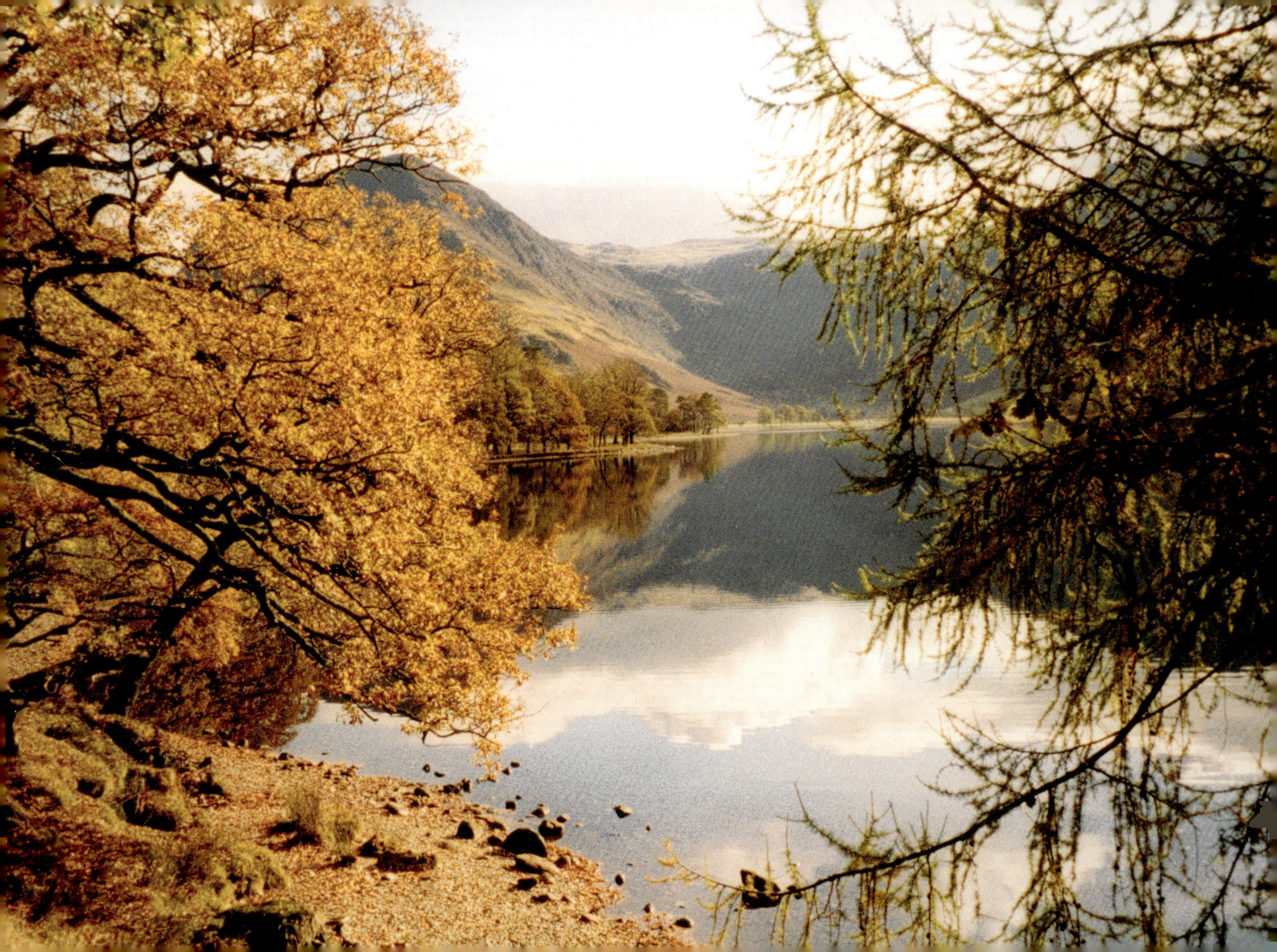

November

The vaulted roof of Summer in the lane
Is tumbling down in ruins at our feet.
Wide beams of light slant through the gloom again
To shine on leaves that now are obsolete.
Yet there is beauty still in their demise,
A gentle feathered floating in their fall;
A strength, with every tiny gust, to rise
And spin like coins, then settle over all.
Grey chiffon scarves of cloud wrap up the sun
And steal along the valleys by the stream;
Chill-fingered comes the night, when day is done,
And dampened roads in orange lamplight gleam,
And, as each shortened autumn day slips by,
November, robed in brown, prepares to die.

December

Of Winter's hoary beard there is no sign.
Is everything in Nature out of tune?
When jasmine's yellow stars begin to shine
One wonders if the spring will come too soon.
New crops are growing in the fresh-tilled fields,
The lilac sports its buds of palest green;
See how last summer's roses new flowers yield,
And many other wonders now are seen.
And yet, the empty trees of winter stand
As though upturned, with tangled roots on high,
And chirping robins sing across the land
And do not seem to mind or wonder why.
So why should we be yearning for the snow,
If our December days in mildness go?

A sudden arctic chill dispels our dreams
As faces burn from icy winds unbound.
Beneath the cloudless skies of morning, gleams
A coverlet of white upon the ground.
The snow glows golden-pink upon the trees,
Each outstretched branch is tinselled in the light,
And gleeful squirrels, on their high trapeze,
Send glitter showers from tiny paws in flight.
Like giant sentinels, the evergreens
Stand silent guard in countryside and town,
The cold moon sails aloft in her demesnes
And crystals shine from Earth's nocturnal crown.
How short the days, how long that Christmas night
When men announced the advent of the Light.

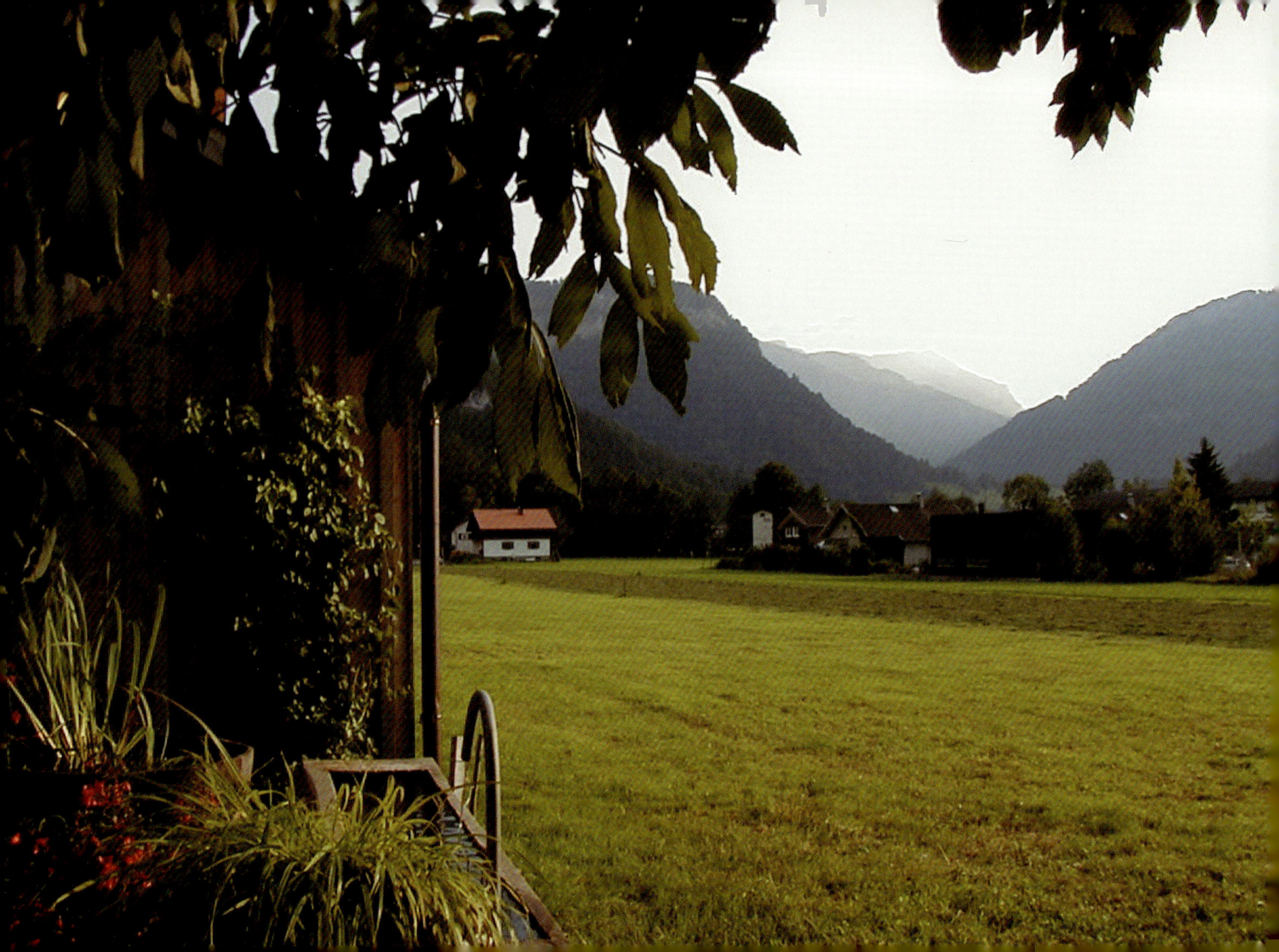

AUSTRIAN SUMMER

Summer in Bregenzerwald 1

Across the wooded slopes the grey clouds drift
Like wreaths of smoke, and pins of rain descend
Upon the sodden earth, where patient cows
Gaze silently upon the flooding plain.
The giant houses wait with studied calm;
In purple-grey their steep-sloped roof-tops gleam,
The gutters overflow in ceaseless streams,
The swollen brook is brown with swirling clay.

But meadows fair now sport their brightest green,
And, flowing down from balconies and sills,
Like many yellow, red and orange suns,
Begonia blooms spread out their shining rays.
Cascades of red and pink geraniums,
Lobelia – dainty, purple, blue and white,
Petunias, with their pink and purple heads
Combine to cheer the travellers on their way.

Summer in Bregenzerwald 2

The mountains overlap their hazy slopes,
Each one more distant and much less defined;
Each stone is burning in the midday heat,
Each far-off tree is stilled in sun and shade.

White, flimsy clouds appear, like wispy ghosts,
Along the margins of a clear, blue sky,
And tiny breezes play along the ground
With clover flowers and dock and gleaming grass.

No sound is heard from insect or from bird;
In heat that's so profound, all nature sleeps.

The church tower clock strikes two, and sends
Its mellow notes across the sun-soaked roofs
To people opening up their village shops
And cyclists spinning down the village street.

The wind is ruffling up the rich, green floor,
Where silent bees are visiting each flower;
And crickets rub their bony legs and sing
While circling birds are calling from on high.

A tractor rolls along a strip of green,
And cuts and turns the hay in tumbled lines.
Bare-footed, wielding three-pronged forks and rakes,
Both men and women follow in its wake
To toss the grass with deft and practised ease.

And when the sun has taken its rich green,
The hay is piled in carts and driven away.

Quite unconcerned about the cars, at five o'clock,
Four cows appear and walk from field to stall –
Their bells mark time with their reluctant gait ;
And, following behind, with quicker steps,
A brown-eyed calf with long and spindly legs
Trots where it will, until it too goes in
And fills the darkened byre with thinner notes.

This is high summer in Bregenzerwald,
Where early morning fields are pearled with dew
And sunlight shimmers on the silver birch,
And where each soul, each little act of grace,
Can make each day a taste of Paradise.

MEMORIES OF TIMES PAST

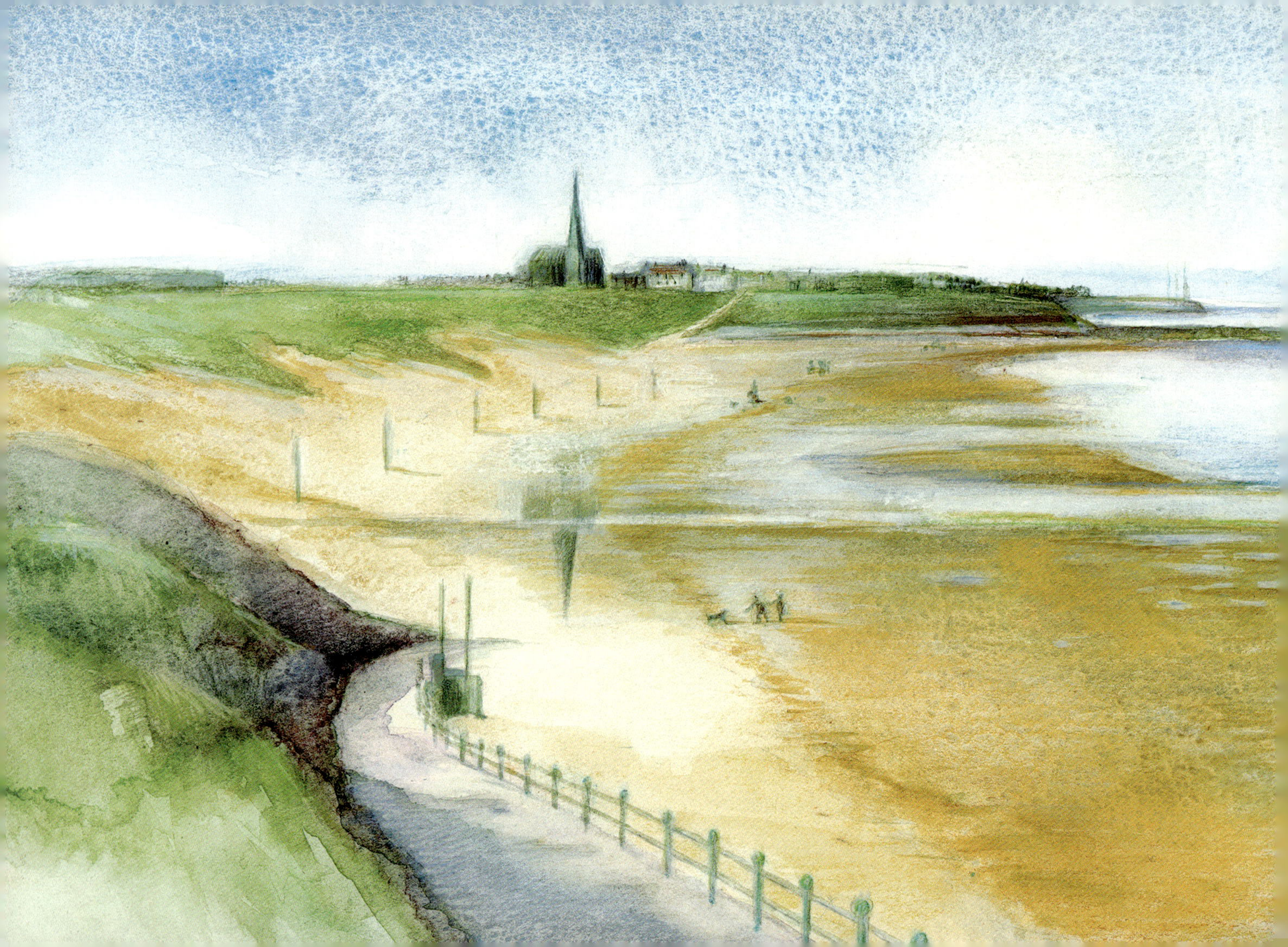

Tynemouth Long Sands

My childhood haunts lie open to the sun
On this September day. The sand is gold
And stretches round and far away to meet
The rocky promontory and the sea,
Whose curving pale-blue satin swathe creeps up
Quite silently upon the empty shore.

And in my mind I conjure other days
When winter blasts whined through the tumbled air
While crashing breakers raced upon the beach
And soaked the land with stinging, salty spray.
To walk along, and lean upon that wind,
That pushed and pulled at legs and clothes and hair,
To feel the glow within damp frozen cheeks,
To taste the salty tang upon the lips
Was wonderful, exhilarating, wild.

And when th'occasional summer day appeared,
With summer's heat, then hundreds would descend
Upon that beach, with buckets, spades and teas,
To paddle in the chilly, gentle waves
Or dig for treasure in the silky sand –
Down, down, until a well was dug
And someone lowered in to wet his toes:
And others went to swing on shuggy-boats,
Or eat ice creams, or jog on pony rides.
Sometimes a mist arose from off the sea,
– A ghostly fret that climbed the busy shore –
The foghorn gave one haunting two-beat moan
And people fled inland to chase the sun,
And left the beach, deserted, to the tide.

On this September day, the sands are bare,
Their beauty changing with each passing hour,
Each mood of wind and water, light and shade.
And now I find my first sharp-focused view
Is added to my bank of memories,
To blend itself into those other days,
Those childhood scenes of fifty years ago.

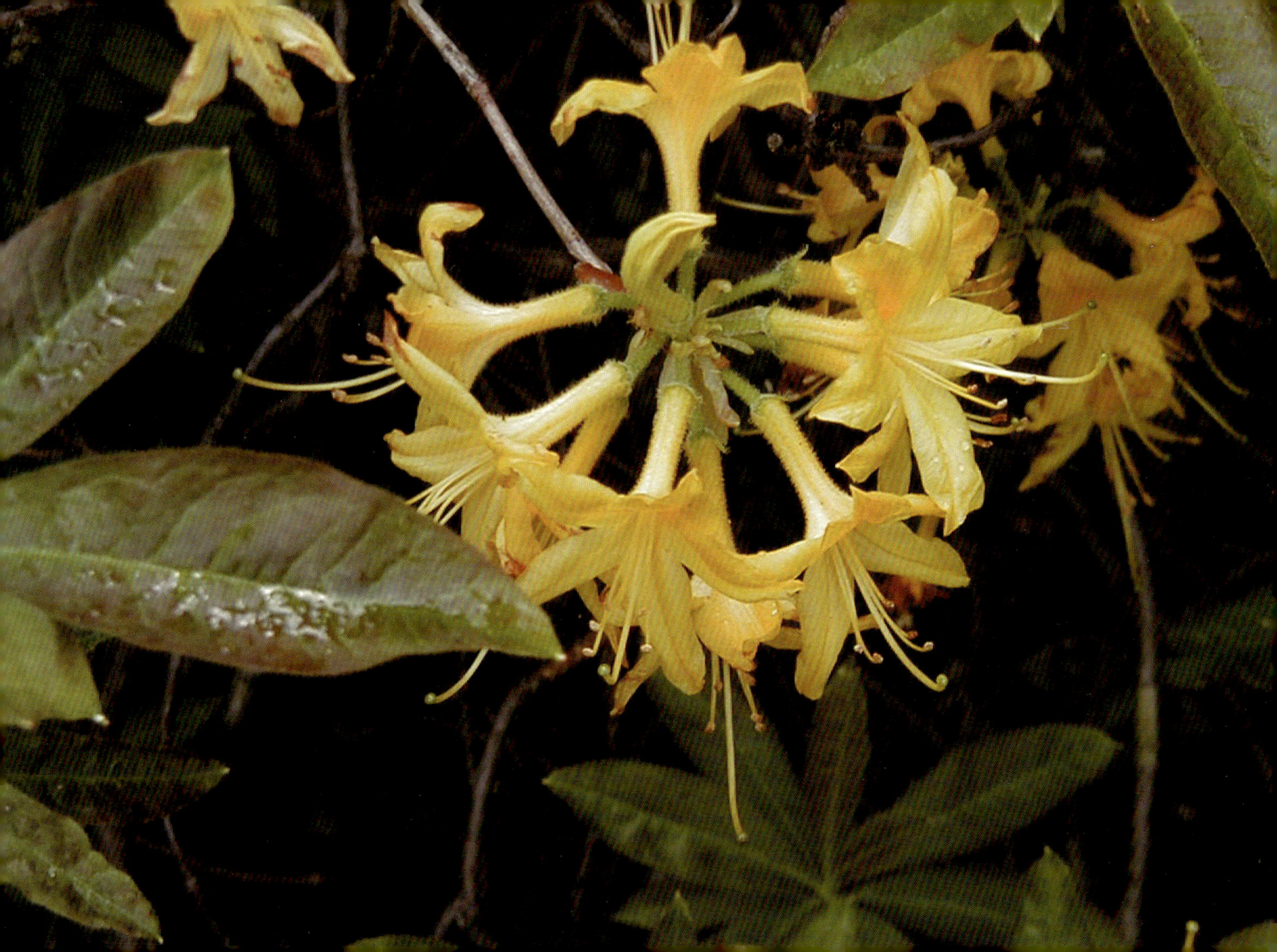

Wentworth Castle

An azalea's golden flowers and pungent scent
Transport me back in time, until I am
But nineteen years of age and revelling
In new delights: the chance to live within
An ancient stately hall; to gaze upon
High, painted ceilings, where, in Summer's sun
Forever shining, pretty maidens trip
And dance, all garlanded with rosy fruit
And flowers, to Pan's eternal pipes;
To mount the Italian Staircase, cool and white,
With statues set in niches in its walls;
To trace a Tudor panel's wooden folds
And look upon the acorn and the rose.

Breathe deeply. See the folly on the hill
Beyond the climbing avenue of limes;
The seat above the archway to the roses' haunt,
Where buds await their turn to grow and bloom:
For it is May.   A gentle, warming breeze
Bears heavenly perfume on its outstretched wings –
An oriental blend, exotic, rich and sweet –
That leads me to a garden set apart,
Where colours flare in oranges and pinks,
Salmon, lemon, peach and apricot,
A deeper pink and one, a darker red,
White, tinged with gold, and each a separate flower
Within a waxen cluster on the stem.

I hear the buzzing of the flies and bees
And feel the warmth of sun upon my head;
I breathe the cloying scent of flowers that glow
Within a bowl of light, all ringed around
With rhododendron leaves and darker trees,
And seem to drown in overwhelming heat.

Now, presently, I stand upon my lawn
And see the glow about one golden bush,
Reminder of young memories to take
And savour and re-live the time that's passed –
Each year, a breath that brings me close to tears.

LIGHT AND JOY

Driving Home

It was in Spring, that, driving eastwards, I
Beheld the Chiltern Hills, a distant smudge
Of blue beneath a purple sky – a sky
Of purple-grey that billowed out like sails.
Behind, the sun was hidden in the west
By clouds more broken and a lighter grey –
Like rippled sand along the ocean floor.

And so it was I neared a village house –
Cream-painted walls beneath a darker roof –
And suddenly the day-shy sun broke through
And cast low beams of light upon that place.

With blinding white, the cottage was transformed.
Against the purple sky it shone and blazed
Upon my eye, and took my breath away.
For now each leaf around was visible;
Each one was etched in gold about the green
In sharp relief. I stopped the car and gazed
And tears prevented me from driving on.

Storm

Can you hear the silence of the birds
When sullen clouds, like sagging shrouds,
Hang over the sunless plain?

Can you hear the rustle of the leaves,
As the torrid heat spirals from its seat
Into the fermenting air again?

Can you see the flicker and the flash,
As the giant switch is tripped
And black becomes white and white turns black?

Can you hear the pause…
Before the CRASH! and the ominous CRACK!
And the rumbling echo
As it answers back?

Can you feel the rain upon your face
And the cool relief in its embrace?

Can you catch a glimpse of the light
Through the watery mist – golden and white?

Can you feel the drips that are shed
By the shivering branches high over your head?

Can you hear the blackbird and thrush
Singing for joy
On top of a bush?

Equinox

From early dawn, the world was washed in grey;
Relentless rain came blowing from the west;
And in the air, upon the wind's high crest,
The birds, like blackened leaves, were borne away;
While, pasted to the road by passing spray,
Lay sodden remnants from the autumn trees.
It seemed that rain and wind would never cease
And darkened clouds were closing in the day.
Then, from the west, a sudden yellow light
Steamed forth, and full upon the hedgerows shone
Which, bathed in lime, their scarlet berries bright
Against the eastern sky, so grey and wan,
Gleamed out. And rainbows spanned the airy height
And long remained, to hearten everyone.

INDEX OF TITLES AND FIRST LINES

Across the wooded slopes the grey clouds drift	38
April	21
An azalea's golden flowers and pungent scent	49
As John the Baptist heralded the Son	16
As lions fight to keep their captured prey	19
August	28
Can you hear the silence of the birds	56
December	34
Driving home	54
Equinox	58
February	18
From early dawn, the world was washed in grey	58
How is it that the birds know when 'tis time	18

How welcome is the warmth, however brief	21
It was in Spring that, driving eastwards, I	54
January	16
July	26
June	24
March	19
May	22
My childhood haunts lie open to the sun	45
November	33
Now is the zenith of the Creator's power	22
October	30
Of Winter's hoary beard there is no sign	34
See how the sun and rain and frost conspire	30

Sensory Perception	13
September	29
September brings a magic of its own	29
Storm	56
Summer in Bregenzerwald 1	38
Summer in Bregenzerwald 2	39
Sun-baked, the cornfields lie like golden sand	28
The early mist gives way to cloudless skies	24
The hay is cut and grass-scent fills the air	26
The mountains overlap their hazy slopes	39
The vaulted roof of summer in the lane	33
Tynemouth Long Sands	45
Wentworth Castle	49
What is this light that flows in radiant streams	13

Acknowledgements

My grateful thanks go to:

Janet Archer, my life-long friend, for her evocative watercolour of Tynemouth Long Sands,

Alastair Hill, for his invaluable help with setting up the text,

Judith Hill, for her wise counsel and skilled proof reading, and

Melanie Ritter, who generously gave up her time to support me whenever I asked for help.